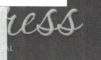

Published by Cinnamon Press
Meirion House
Glan yr afon
Tanygrisiau
Blaenau Ffestiniog
Gwynedd, LL41 3SU
www.cinnamonpress.com

ISBN: 978-1-907090-42-4
British Library Cataloguing in Publication Data. A CIP record for this book can be obtained from the British Library.

Designed and typeset in Palatino by Cinnamon Press.
Cover from original photograph © Anne-Marie Glasheen 2007
www.glasheen.co.uk - used with kind permission.
Cover design by Jan Fortune-Wood.
Printed in Poland

The publisher acknowledges the support of Arts Council England Grants for the Arts.

LOTTERY FUNDED

Cinnamon Press is represented in the UK by Inpress Ltd www.inpressbooks.co.uk and in Wales by the Welsh Books Council www.cllc.org.uk.

Acknowledgements

Thanks are due to the editors of the following magazines and anthologies, who published some of these poems or earlier versions of them: *Connections, French Literary Review, Frogmore Papers, Horizon Review, Images of Women* (Arrowhead Press, 2006), *Interpreter's House, My Mother Threw Knives* (Second Light Publications, 2006), *Poetry London, The Rialto, Seam, Seeking Refuge* (Cinnamon Press, 2010), *Kaleidoscope: An Anthology of Poetry Sequences* (Cinnamon Press, 2011), *The SHOp, The Shuffle Anthology* (The Shuffle Press, 2008), *Did I Tell You?: 131 Poems for Children in Need* (Categorical Books, 2010), *Writing Women*.

Mahler 9 won first prize in the 2009 Troubadour Poetry Prize competition. *When You've Gone* won first prize in the 2008 Canterbury Poet of the Year competition. *Collector* was a prize winner in the 2007 Peterloo Competition and *Through a Glass* was placed third in the 2007 Canterbury Poet of the Year competition. *Birth Rights* received a special commendation in the National Poetry Competition.

I am indebted to Steve Anthony, Anne Berkeley, Claire Crowther, Jenny Lewis, Rhona McAdam, Geraldine Paine, Lynne Rees, Robert Stein, Siriol Troup and Tamar Yoseloff for their critical input and inspiration. My gratitude also to the MPhil staff and students at the University of Glamorgan, particularly Gillian Clarke and Sheenagh Pugh, and to members of the TRPW workshop.

Special thanks to Anne-Marie Glasheen, who allowed me to use her photograph for the cover.

This book owes everything to my family's unfailing love and support.

Contents

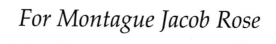

For Montague Jacob Rose

From the Dark Room

Collector

She started small, a mouse head, sharp folds of bone
pincered in a snap. The structures gleamed
as she polished them, arctic, rococo.

Soon random finds were not enough—a badger gleaned
from the forest, the long-toothed snout of her dolphin
washed up on the sand, a facsimile of some power tool—

so she graduated to roadkill, cutting off heads, waiting.
She found a snowy owl on the tarmac,
fanned out like spilt milk, watched for months

as the head shrank, the eyeballs collapsed
into yellow craters and the beak whittled down
to a cipher. It was beautiful to see things becoming

the essence of themselves, losing
their padding, the frippery of fat and muscle.
No more blues and pinks, maroons and browns,

just the calcium-cold symmetry of white.
Now she stares in the mirror.
Her bones press against the pale drum of skin

like the spines of an open umbrella. She is aspiring,
patient, as she waits for her body to claim
this spare perfection, for nature to finish its work.

Rare Old

The glaciers shifted with music
too high, too low, for the human ear,
a music of sensation, and ice formed
beneath Shackleton's hut, packing
its crumpled hexagons about the crates,
holding his abandoned whisky tight
as sand or rock. Antarctica waits
for the new wave of explorers, armed
with syringes, drills and picks
to extract the extinct liquor
protected by the freeze.
       The land is breached.
The milder waters of ancient lakes
have left behind fossils of ostracods,
icebergs topple into the melt
and glaciers rot. The chilled terrain
will be forced to deliver its message—
yesterday's peat, the blend of centuries,
brought into the damage of light.

Globe

Some show lightscapes of cities tracked
by satellite at dark, others are inflatable

or lit within. Mine was metal,
cratered by carelessness. I'd frame it

with my hands—the way lovers later
would still my face—then make it turn

to a carousel of pinks, blues, reds:
countries we coloured differently,

contours hollowing as the sea bit in.
I didn't wonder then what swelled

inside holding the surface taut,
or what might ooze if the egg

of the Earth were cracked, light
hatching from the world's blown sphere.

Hemispheres

From here, you can see the baked roofs
of the town, a family of blue and brown tiles
overlaid, protecting their neighbours;
metal curtains mist front doors, canaries sing
their caged music and a radio plays.
A girl lies on her bed opposite, listening
to songs that make her long

for elsewhere. My sister rings
to say it's snowing at home, the sky dizzy
with flakes, the sea cold slate.
The children are in the garden packing
the cold into a man. They are living
their frozen afternoon in the hours
this sundial has misplaced, the slippage

between hemispheres. Telephone wires
strung from roof to roof are iced with light
and the air smells of dust; in the resonant shade
of the church bell, house martins are building
basketwork nests, coming back, time
and again, flattening against the walls,
sliding the dark around themselves, arriving.

Taking Flight

Perhaps you stand
on the indeterminate rim,
hills below and above,

wind fills your dress, billows
in your sleeves, lifting
the material of you like a kite;

you turn your sight away
from the contours of the land,
green of dead water, dark terraces,

a house, perhaps,
its roof a dull mosaic, smoke
from the chimney lifting, breaking,

and you take to the air,
whole and beautiful,
recalling, as you broach the sky,

the feel in your hands
of a small brown bird,
wings stilled, heart labouring,

when you took it from the room
and, palms splayed,
offered it to the free air,

you remember now its burr
of wings, joyous applause,
ascending into the blue.

Migration

i.m. Elisabeth Ganne

She looks asleep in her chair by the window,
her parted lips still and a speckle of blood
on her white cheek like a beauty spot.

Outside, the trees rend the air like women
paid to follow the painted sarcophagus, wailing
into the wild wind, sending birds spiralling up.

The screensaver hurls a snowfall of stars
at the empty office chair and the monitor frames
a darkness black as Anubis. On her desk, a scatter

of lexicons and books, the picture of a ba bird perched
on the prow of Ra's solar bark heading east.
The *Book of the Dead* lies open at Spell 86:

she shall go out into the day, she shall not be turned
away at any gate in the realm of the dead
and she shall assume the shape of a swallow.

Glass Books

Those who know how to decipher water's braille
in rain, can read these sheaves. Pick one up, feel

the crystallisation of ice under your fingers, furrow
and pock of hairline cracks. Nothing you can do

to salvage these drowned letters, their electrics
doused, light dulled to a sheen. Information is

now transparent. You can only huff on the gloss
and hope that something will rise in the fog.

Sanatorium

Mosquito hour. You wake to wings
drilling at your ear, but the dream stays—

the silent screen popping, its mirror
offered to the sky, clouds moving,

trees lacing the confines
of the glass, a burst of sunlight.

The man in the white coat smiles;
his hand comes up like a stop sign,

palm out, mirror ingrained, blinking.
You don't recognise the face

looking back, though it tilts
its head when you cock yours.

Familiarity hovers at the crease of the lips,
but you're lost, your only way out

that round window, its vista
a mute world feathered with light.

Lost

Like a limb or the blank squint
of an eye, unafraid of sun or grit,
the things that are gone

are gone. Their ache is reliable,
resilient as steel through concrete,
preventing the collapse into sleep

or starting you from dreams
like a tractor in the dark narrows
of morning; there are no surprises.

What terrifies now is joy–
the tall structure still standing,
its supple roll and sway.

The Seamstress at Queille

She stands by the pool
watching the girl break

the clouds' reflection
over and over—

soon it will be time
to bid her change

the skin of water
for satin that will trail

down crumbling steps
behind her like a shadow

to the cool chapel,
air clothing her arms

in gooseflesh, vows resonant
in the domed silence.

When the invisible sun dips,
the seamstress will come again

to mar her pure creation.
Shearing off the train

with mottled, attar-scented
hands, she'll free the bride

from her fluid serpent
so she can tramp the dirt

to the beat of the tambour
in the lantern light, white roses

frothing down the wall,
petals hemmed with brown.

Miss Beckett

The curtain strokes the loose skin
of her shoulders as she wakes
to days long and familiar
as razor shells, to puddled sand
between her toes. She walks slowly
into colder weather. Among pine needles
she finds the skull of a rabbit,
licked clean and beaked like a bird.
She puts it on the shelf: the kind of promise
that will be kept. Nights are shivered
by the shriek of foxes. In the white
silence of morning, she crumbles pellets
of dung, acrid as smelling salts,
to still her fears. Then the sun stirs
stone, and colour runs like flame
from edge to centre. The year turns over
like an old engine and idles at her door.
She lifts the curtain from her face as a bride.

Through a Glass

I

Sometimes, at night, from a train,
when the curve of the track
brings you rocking past back yards
and rooms pour out their heart,
you might see an embrace, a fight,
in the blue cell of a lounge
or glimpse a table set
for the silent falling to
of the lonely. Illuminated,
they stand against the dark:
a girl cleaning teeth, a man washing up,
a mother kissing her children,
the walk between one room and the next,
the daily drawing of curtains.

II

As night came in slowly like mist off the sea—
blowing through streets, turning on lamps,
lighting windows into peepshows—
my father would sneak into the back
of the flat where he grew up,
share field glasses with his dad.
They'd wait in the dark, like children
for fireworks, to see the woman appear
in the window of the next block, watch
as she unbuttoned, unzipped, stepped
into a pin-up of lace-cupped breasts
and long, long legs. She glowed against the light,
perhaps humming to the wireless, so close,
so real, he could almost feel her heat.

III

This afternoon, the sea was a blue hem
to the spring light and the clock tower
a timeless needle. Two streets away
and two floors down, two girls chased
each other in and out of the sash, dark
as deep water, their filmy dresses flickering
like sunlight on fish backs. I couldn't hear
their shrieks, smell the factor-50 sheen
of their shoulders. Now it's late,
their home looks empty, and although
I imagine their minty snuffle as they curl
round sucked fingers in sleep,
for all I know, they were a conjuring
in the reflected garden of a deserted house.

Oradour-sur-Glâne

In the standing church,
                    a pram crouches
          flat by the altar, a dumb cricket.
The melted tongue
                    of the great bell
     lies
on the flags near the confessional.

Burnt-out Renaults acquire
                    a crochet of rust
          in garages of air. The sockets
of their headlamps, dull
                    O's like choir mouths,
     rest
on arches above blind axles.

The Singer machine, low voice
                    of the humdrum,
          keeps mum. No thread of song,
no hands to feed
                    and guide the cloth.
     Weeds
and the sun telling time by its dial.

From St Mark's Campanile

The piazza is a stage
two hundred feet below. Small figures like performing fleas
      follow a line of dance, light on their toes,

their raggedy tango frayed
by the rival strains of café bands. Pigeon calls and pleas
      from watching tourists don't disturb his pose,

legs together, arms outstretched,
a gilded angel glistening in the sun. *Amore,*
      Amore, a woman behind him cries,

but he seems stone on the edge,
focused on his enterprise. He casts his T-shirt away.
      It rides the currents, warning passers-by

to look up, move back. His cue
comes soon enough. At the clock bell's clamour, the pigeons reel.
      He takes a deep breath and closes his eyes.

On the second stroke of noon,
he rises on tiptoe and, gracefully, with the third peal,
      he flies.

Getting his Wings

Don't think about it, his pals
had told him, think about anything but—
Hitler, his checklist for take-off,
the greasy interlocking parts of his gun—
anything to avoid being done too soon,
so he led the girl to an empty hangar
at the edge of base and laid her
giggling on the cold concrete
as the music from the dance fell away.

Propping his arms either side,
he eased himself down,
eyes fixed on the dark line
of his horizon, the body
beneath him a distraction,
its green silk a swathe of field
in the full moon, hair a river
of platinum spilling through it,
marcasite the lights of a small town.

Cousin Dickie

The first Brylcreem Boy to advertise the Bounce,
his slicked-back charm smiling from all the papers,
his dance routine with George Raft in the clubs,
his girls, his Sobranies, he took after my uncle,

the margarine king, but the factory wasn't for him.
He owned a gold Ford V8, the only car the kids in my street
got to see up close: walnut dash, leather seats,
he'd cruise me round Stepney, pointing out women.

Though he married after the war, it guttered
in smoky nights, his chrome lighter always snapping
at some offered cigarette. He finished in a showroom
selling cars, a connoisseur of fine chassis to the last.

When I picture him, though, I see that grin as he circled
the clock tower on Stepney Green where the Blackshirts
were mustering—*England for the English* punched out
in dark armbands and lightning flash. Round and round

he crawled in first, his hand jammed hard against the horn,
blaring over *Jews are the Financiers of Evil*, daring Mosley's lot
to make him stop, the smell of hair cream on his fingers
as he cuffed my cheek, a curl of sweet smoke hanging at his ear.

Travelling Light

I

It's usual to start with edges,
piecing together a frame
crammed with flowers or mountains,
but this puzzle is different, obscure—
indigo veined with branches, dun shadows
below and to the sides, pressing in on a car,
two beams, fierce against the dark—
so it's easier to do headlamps first,
sifting the box for flashes of yellow.
There are gaps though. The jigsaw is old,
a scree of cardboard laid out many times
on the table for a vision of night speed;
a family pastime filling young evenings
to the soundtrack of Radio Two.
The pieces are bent, lined and delicate
as old skin; many are lost,
like my mother's gentle duets
with Sinatra or Satchmo as she cast
around for another piece to fill
the rift between outline and picture,
light taking shape in the foreground.

II

The mirror blooms with light,
overtaking me. It displaces
the easy darkness above my eyes
like a slide snapping down
in a pocket viewer,
replacing the screen with a child
I recognise as myself
but only from albums
and family tale-telling—
anecdotes from the dark room
of childhood—not from being four
under a beach tap, naked
and brash before the camera.
And if I search the lit mirror above,
I find only adult eyes looking back,
a sequence of pictures frozen
to a lie—the grizzling pain
of sand towelled into the skin
is held at bay by white borders
until swallowed by the dark.

III

The mirror above my eyes
is a rectangle of obsidian,
an unlit shaft leading down;
it's as if the past has turned
hard and black like the road behind
that pours through the mirror,
solidifying in the cold;
all things pass under
and beyond my reach
of light, disappearing
like the catseyes: feldspar
embedded in a basaltine road.
Beneath this waste of tufa
is a city I knew before the eruption
of time. It's preserved
by layer on layer of ash flakes
and mud: the track of days hardened
to a coating too thick to penetrate.
Excavation might yet uncover
treasures caged in a clutch of bone —
half-shelled eggs, centuries old,
rolling among stone cakes
and split amphorae: the debris
of events gone under the dust.

IV

Edging into a roundabout, I'm brought up sharp
by the plate of the car in front. I'm tailing
two decades of history, as if the spin of wheels
has shot me back. Those silhouettes
could be my parents—any moment the face
that grins, full of teeth, from sideboard frames,
will pop up in the rear window to make friends;
they could be me and my father—pronouncements
on sex, love, the Pill, banging back and forth
with the wipers; or perhaps I am the driver,
my dark passenger the cause of slammed doors
and wheelspin getaways—a trained eye could read
a map of love on the back seat, find the earring
that pairs with the diamante drop I now wear
on a chain. Get in, and the driver's seat would know
the length of my leg, just as my thigh recalls
the warmth of your hand down a dark stretch of road.

V

Through the full beam, rain
falls as glitter in winter's dome,
shaken to disturb the settled peace.
Christmas was always a feast
of refracted lights: candles wavering
in the eight-branched menorah
beside the tinsel tree, a glass ball
sent spinning into splinters
by a cat's paw, Polaroid flashes
flattening laughter.
Like beads of rain caught
as the light transforms them,
each scene yields only an image
then soaks into the road and is gone.

Fox Crossing

Not so strange, a flash
of fox, standing by the side
of the Westway, no more strange

than the deserted carriageway,
the yolky light, the city
running silent. I wanted

to stop the car, bundle her
into my arms like laundry,
her pelt uncompromising,

take her to the safety of grass
far from the verge, the killing
speed, watch her furled in sleep.

I drove on, eyes fixed on the rear-view —
the inquisitive forager stepping high,
paws testing the asphalt, like snow.

Sample

I'm driving to the hospital
along a skein of water,
your DNA in my pocket—
two hundred million blueprints
motoring round a plastic pot
nested in a woollen sock
the tender blue of thrushes' eggs.

If this rain continues
and the world goes under again—
fields, churches and cities
roofed by a formless sea—
I'll still count as a pair
for the new ark. Bearing you
in my hand, I'd step aboard,
take to bed in the hold.

Scientists would come
to claim you as I lay curled
to keep you living. Supercooled
in liquid nitrogen, you'd be
cloned back to me, child
and husband, when the waters fell
and the dove returned.

This motile spoonful,
fertile as silt,
holds such power.
No more though
than a formula for a man,
a cloudy fluid tilting
in its crucible, waiting
to become.

Minute Waltz

And isn't it funny, like they say,
how much you want something
if your chances are reduced,
and you're driving along the highway,
wrinkles squinting at the rear-view,
hands all knuckles and veins on the wheel,
when, as if to add insult, you're told
by the DJ that the music pattering
under wheel thrum and wind noise
which, you realise only now, had got you
picturing girls in pink tutus with ribbon straps
over lark-boned shoulders, their bellies pouting,
the music you'd half been humming
was Frédéric Chopin's 'Menopause'.

Magnolia

Sunday afternoon.
British Summer Time has just begun
and you're walking that path again,
thinking how it might have been
married to the bearded architect
from Doune. You'd have children in tow
by now, questioning the bruised rainbow
of the canal, the scuffling hedgerow.

As you trudge,
the fields of loam, worms and cowpats seem
to converge on a point, twisting like bath water,
carrying the babies out of sight, fat smiles
thinning in the grass, time wearing on,
the useless moon on its back.

The beds are crowded
with nursery colours, daffodils, hyacinths
and pansies, and you're left to cope
with the tang of cut grass, an ice-cream van
chiming through the streets, the prolific magnolia,
its torches sweet and erect.

Poseidon Burning

after a pyrotechnical fire sculpture by Robert Bradford

He took shape slowly that November,
hammer, staple-gun, nails summoning
a barrelled driftwood divinity bulked
on the shingle, a warship waiting on the tide.
We had come to see him burn, watch
the torching of this cobbled god
before he could call up earthquakes, incite
the sea to damage, implant his seed.

The flames feathered his back and legs
bridging the long strides to the water's edge
where his downturned toes dipped and crabbed.
His skull was limned in fire, his sockets glared
until the air itself burned, hopping with light.
Transfixed, we refused to turn and run
in the escaping crowds, you hugging the secret
in your belly, your upturned face glorious
in the wild golden ritual of ash.

The Labour Room

I may have thought how strange it was
that the sister I used to balance
on hands and feet for acrobatic shows
in the lounge, the little girl
who used to dance on the wide ledge
of the bedroom window with next door's boys,
was now spread out on this trestle
her swollen sex every shade of maroon;

but when the flamboyant red parted
like a vertical eyelid and the blind white crown
of my niece appeared, when she lay
between my sister's slack knees,
bluish and floury, her cry as mundane
and miraculous as you could wish;

and when I watched the midwife draw down
the perfect lobes of the placenta
with its marbled cord, exotic as a water lily,
for that moment I understood everything
and the world hung ripe in my reach.

Birth Rights

This room is full of daughters
punctuating the bloodline.
She is the latest: the point
where centuries pool
their wisdom, their suffering.

The breast she draws on
is old as Russia or Poland,
the milk rounding her belly pumps
from a heartbeat foreign
as the slow cold of the *shtetl*.

This is where it has ended:
through the luck of the chosen, despite
the luck of the chosen,
this blood stops here, briefly,
in this pastel waiting room.

Mimosa

My study reels
with their marzipan smell,
fluffy yellow heads

tightening daily
until hard and diminished.
This slow dying

has them exiled
from the living room:
he hates their sweetness.

I recall bouquets,
holed cellophane erupting
with fuzzy constellations

lighting the lounge
in flared vases
with abstract patterns.

My mother
must have worked miracles
to keep them alive.

Hard Skin

She rests her legs on mine. I massage
her bunions, rub the lump on top of her foot.
She kneads my protesting arches, the corrugated bone
of my ankle, broken years ago and prone to aches.

I slide my nail under the white crusts
of skin on her toe tips, lifting wide strips, small flakes
like dried glue, worrying at the tiny tags
around her toenails, the brittle scales on her heels.

She huffs at the length of my nails, seizes
a pair of scissors and prunes them, twisting
my feet this way and that, brusque and careful,
though we both sometimes draw blood.

On this sofa we are intimate as lovers
with the callused contours of each other's feet,
mine accruing the mottled patina of hers,
the papery instep, the armoured ball.

Maribárbola

after Las Meninas *by Velázquez*

Tricked out in green
velvet, lace, clutching
a small volume
bigger than her fist,
she stands in the margin,
face flat, resigned,
reddened in the light,
her dark squatness
ballast for the blonde
Infanta's cream skin,
half smile.

She waits on the side
for nothing, fortunate
to be wedded
to this estate, knowing
she's as valued
as a mastiff to a mistress
born to be painted
beautiful, each blemish
brushed out, a palette
of oils and pigments
shaving her infant form.

Hoops of baleen
beneath her farthingale
are kind to her
dumpy legs, pleats

of stomach hanging
like melted wax—
she has no need
for the polite
constraint of a corset,
her breath at liberty
to come and go.

Caravaggio's Virgin

I hadn't met anyone like him before.
All I had to do was play dead—much easier
than pacing the narrow dark
round Piazza Navona, heels stabbing
at the stairs of bridges, arches strained.
 My red shoes glowed like lanterns
in the corner of the room, my bare feet froze;
I couldn't breathe for the reek of pigments,
the scarlet drapes blooming
in the candlelight, taking all the air.
 He told me red was the only true colour,
the colour of sex, joked about the death
of the Virgin in a shift of reds, the symbolism
of bare feet, mocking the pilgrims on their way
to sanctuary. There is no deliverance,
he said, no Assumption.
 He wouldn't show me at first,
the canvas turned against the wall.
He coloured my skin instead, a flush
of heat livening the grain of my body
beneath the canopy, his strokes sure.
 He said he loved me
but he was a liar—look at me
lying there, bloated, hair dull,
hemmed in by a bevy of old men,
any fallen woman fished from the Tiber,
soles blackened by walking the streets.

Chinese

Over the chilli prawns,
she tells him
she isn't wearing knickers,
lets him feel
the flesh above her knee,
then move higher;

sticky spare ribs and curls
of seaweed lie
on the platter between them.

When you've gone

I won't waste time searching
the lightless rooms of the wreck
that went down, refusing
to surface, holding my breath.
Instead, I'll lift your surfboard
from its high wooden cradle,
drag it with the rig seaward
and, there, on an edge of shingle,
assemble the sail and jib, insert
the dagger, walk it into the swell,
ignoring the water's numb hurt.
I'll clamber on, stand, tug the sail
upright to catch an off-shore breeze,
then, leaning on the wind, I'll leave.

The Wreck of the Alba

after Alfred Wallis

Masts, decks, jetty, hills, dulled to old metal,
sunlessness, the mineral land, squalled wet.
Coal in the holds, iron in the stones, no light
from the lighthouse; the vessel is divided
by salt water churning like chyme.

It's a dirty drowning, thick water filling eyes,
ears, lungs, like off-milk, rancid curds blueing
the periphery. Things lost flash by, dropping
into the depths. You cannot keep a hold —
they plummet through the water like dark boots.

MRI

Like the wind, unseen
but for sand strimming the beach,

or faith coaxing blood
from the eyes of a saint,

there is a force working
beneath the skin, noticeable

only by what it moves,
the miracles it performs.

When it leaves, you're left
with a skeleton ringing its lack,

a white and black image
of a brain, its high cupola frescoed

with light, a large dark moth
fluttering in the dome.

Searching for "Sue Rose"

None of them is me. I'm not
the shaping mind behind stone gardens;
I haven't caught a solar eclipse
on film, or juggled a helix
of planets to chart a life; I am not
the cited fighter pilot, the Christian,
the dietician, the midwife advising
women to belly dance their babies
into the world;
              and it wasn't me
who switched off the machine breathing
for itself alone that morning in March
when the snow had barely gone and the cold
crept into an old man's bones.

Rising

Lying
on a sheeted foam plinth on the bed,
relentless
as stone, he's worn from struggling,
dark veins
ticking under his skin with the effort
of breath,
tendons coiling and releasing as his hot
hands flex.

His head
is coronated with coarse sparks of hair,
his throat,
chest, belly are scrubby with down,
arrowing
to the V of his groin, the warm amber
pouch
of the catheter hidden. He is sexless,
angelic.

He sits
on the edge as we wash away the faint smell
of living,
sponge the crusting sites of new sores.
His skin
is spanned by galaxies—red dwarfs,
black holes.
Brown nebulae cloud his pallor. He has become
our universe.

He tries
to stand, tethered by our hands. His shoulders
are curtains,
folded wings of flesh that lengthen and feather
on rising.
Shakily, he is acquiring the wisdom of Enoch,
waiting
to be dressed in raiments of flame and helped
to his throne.

After

So many shocks hammer at my pulse—
the old answerphone message, charred air
in the crematorium, the smoky kiss
of peat whisky. His white stone shoulder.
Picking him up from the parlour in a bag.

Whisky and Ice

My blood stands poisonous as salt,
pillared in the belled vaults
of my body, a sea frozen into stasis
at 80 degrees below, numb to your lips,
your fingers, the warmth of your tongue.
Like an Arctic explorer carrying the sun
in a flask, you siphon a sip
from your mouth to mine in a kiss,
hoping this ray of heat might start
a thaw, but the spirit sets hard
in the geometries of ice;
the chill invades, abides,
killing the savour and smell of peat,
my father's goodnight kiss, my grief.

Heavy Elements

Lead

Too slight for his clothes, he was filled
with lead the midnight we arrived
to find him half on, half off the bed.

The next morning, flopped forward
on the bedside stool, arms dragging, head
on knees, it took a man's strength

to Heimlich him back—the younger body
a winch, legs rollers, torso a pallet—till both men
lay side by side on the tangled sheets.

Mercury

This death runs like quicksilver
through the blood branching
beneath her skin, withering her

ring by ring. She's sinking
under the pressure, a barometer,
lower than ever before.

Her widow's hump crests
as her body bends like a cane
under the burden of vacant air.

Oxygen

My passenger seat is empty. No more
converters, blocky as valve amps, huffing
their square music into our hall.

No more hospitals, tank shouldered
to navigate the hostile air, canula pipe
twining round handbrake and gearstick

like the convolvulus he used to rip up
by the handful, face beaded with sweat,
as he unbent to catch his breath.

Carbon

In this urn, his new shape,
his shapelessness—frame, stomach, liver, lungs
returned to their essential elements—

five pounds' weight of variegated gravel:
grey charcoal, yellow unburned trabecular bone,
white ash and black carbon, waiting to join

hers in a hotter furnace, forming diamonds
for their daughters, fashioned from high heat
and pressure, hard enough to last.

Halcyon

Strange vigil this: azure, cobalt, celadon
inhabit the landscape, but the blues catching
my eye are scraps of plastic flapping
in the cold, not a message from beyond.
Common birds can be ignored—a kingfisher
is what he promised as proof of afterlife,
but the trees are drab; springtime ice
crusts the earth and waves crest the shore.
Look there though—a flick of orange and white
in the bands of cloud: the clearing sky yields
the span of a halcyon, her back parallel
to the blue. Bearing her dead mate in flight,
her unseen progress over the sea's salt fields
uncouples the wind's plough, calms the water's swell.

Making a Gem

I will measure out their ash
in the kitchen scales like gritty flour,
combining his and hers, light and dark

perhaps, agitating the urns gently
as the red needle edges to the black line—
exactly two hundred grams—

and pour the mixture into a bag
for the short drive to the post office,
pensioners' queue, special delivery.

Then a hot oven, three hundred centigrade,
relentless as the earth's core, baking
their captured carbon to pure graphite—

unique elements, sealed by steel forgings
in a crucible. Days of pressure will refine
them slowly, forcing change. Matter breaks

under such forces, atoms crystallise
and molecules bond to form stone,
fancy blue or yellow, octahedral, in the rough.

Mahler 9

Looking beyond the contrabassoon, timps, strings,
I see you suddenly in the second row, chin supported
by your thumb, index admonishing your cheek,
crook of your third finger beneath your nose
and I can almost feel your hot dry clasp.
You can't be here, of course, listening
to these shining violins sawing farewell,
you whom we keep as ash and celluloid
in high rooms, but my eyes would have you there,
shock of white hair, bushy brows, eyes pained
by this modern noise; the solo flute struggles
against the loud, white wind of the conductor's work,
the man in the second row moves his hand,
and his mouth is a stranger as the music tips
into its climax and the bass clarinet lows
beneath the brass, saying we all carry our dead
with us on a quest for new homes, the klezmer dance
in our head propelling us forward, the fiddle pulling us back.

Arrival

It would be like this: I'd wheel my case
past blank officials, the light stronger
than my eyes can take, dazed
and blinking in the swell of strangers
casting around for a familiar face
as we pass the gate to the other side;
it's so hard to go on keeping faith
after so many years without a sign.
But you're there, patiently standing by
to take me home—I knew you'd wait.
We both smile as your eyes meet mine
and you raise your hand in a little wave.
It's all behind me now, the guilt, the blame—
I make my way to you and am reclaimed.